THE APOSTATE?

A PASSOVER STORY.

WHO IS THE APOSTATE?

A PASSOVER STORY.

WHO IS THE APOSTATE?

A Passover Story.

TRANSLATED FROM THE GERMAN

OF THE

REV. ADOLPH SAPHIR, B.A.

LONDON:

THE RELIGIOUS TRACT SOCIETY,

56 PATERNOSTER ROW, 65 ST. PAUL'S CHURCHYARD,
AND 164 PICCADILLY.

Translated by the Rev. John Kelly.

WHO IS THE APOSTATE?

A PASSOVER STORY.

First Evening.

THE reading of the Hagadah [1] was over,
and they were sitting round the table in
confidential intercourse. The young married
couple kept the feast for the first time in their
own house, and had invited some friends to
spend the evening with them. On the left of
the mistress of the house sat an old man with

[1] The collection of Prayers, Hymns, Scriptures, etc.,
referring to the Exodus, which is read in Jewish house-
holds at the Passover feast.

deep-set eyes, half closed—a tried friend of the family, who indeed, as they thought, had not kept up with the times, but whose sound understanding and true-heartedness were ample compensation for his old-fashioned ideas. Opposite to him sat a slim young man, with long fair hair, who looked pertly and knowingly out of his spectacles, that did not seem to have got accustomed to rest on his nose. This young man was the brother of the mistress of the house. He was then a student of philosophy —what he was destined to become will be duly recorded in the history of his time. The third guest was an early friend of the master of the house. He had passed many years abroad, and had recently returned to Germany. He had taken the little sister of the philosopher on to his knee, and asked her if she knew why they celebrated the feast that day.

"Of course I know," she answered, quickly; "the Passover is kept every year."

He was about to explain to her how people were often ignorant of a matter, and remained in ignorance of it just because it was of yearly recurrence ; but the old friend of the family interrupted him.

"How impressive and elevating is this Passover feast!" he said. "It reminds us in so lively a manner of the past centuries, it enables us to realize our oneness with our fathers, who have observed it from year to year in all the countries of the world whither they have been scattered ; nay more, we see in spirit the wonderful exodus of Israel out of the land of bondage."

"That is all very beautiful and poetical," suggested the young philosopher ; "but the account given in the books of Moses of the passage of the Red Sea and other miracles, is inconsistent with a sound understanding, or, rather, with pure reason," he continued, either not observing or disregarding the signs and nods of his sister. "There is no harm in that, however ; we must learn to distinguish between the kernel and the shell ; the underlying idea is true ; and the ceremony, although rather tiresome to us youngsters, may have a good moral effect."

"Dearest Abraham, I don't understand you," said the old man. "When the shops are shut, and a general holiday is kept throughout Germany on the 18th of October, do the people celebrate an idea or a fact? Do people mean to say that lawless power can never prevail, or that on the 18th of October, 1813, the French were beaten at Leipzig? That is just the way in which I look at our Passover; more enduring than a monument of brass, it publishes the wonderful deliverance of Israel from Egypt; and no other nation can show so ancient and venerable a festival."

There was a deep earnestness in his words; but the tone in which they were uttered betrayed excitement and irritation, as if the old man felt that he, the only greybeard in the company, stood alone alike in his religious opinions and his national feelings.

"I agree with you perfectly," said the stranger, after a few moments; "but allow me briefly to lay my view of the Passover, and how it should be kept, before you. You will grant that a thing is not holy and venerable merely because it is hoary from age. Cain and Abel were contemporaries; from the beginning there were in the world worshippers of God, children of truth, and worshippers of idols, children of darkness. Antiquity hallows nothing—it does not impress everybody; look at our friend here, for instance; he could perhaps tell us of Chinese festivals that are more ancient than ours, or at least as old. But what comes from God is holy —what God has commanded and instituted is venerable : the Passover feast is holy and venerable to me, not because my forefathers have kept it for thousands of years, but because it declares what the Lord God did this night— how He redeemed His people. But I maintain more than this. Useless, vain, and blasphemous— yes, honoured sir, I must express my conviction— blasphemous is the way in which this Passover is for the most part observed among us Jews, because the majority think, at most, of the fathers, and of the thousands of years of our existence, and not of God the Lord, because the majority suppose that nothing is known of God in general, and have a God of nature and of reason, but not the God of Israel, who brought them out of Egypt. Only he who feels as the Jews once felt in Egypt—the nearness of God as their Father and King, who forgives their sins and atones for them, and regards them as His chosen children—only such an one keeps the Passover in reality and integrity. But where is there such a Jew?"

The whole company fixed a look of inquiry and astonishment on the stranger, as he took a little pamphlet out of his pocket, and requested permission to read an extract which might perhaps make his position clearer, as he feared he might not have expressed himself plainly enough. He read the following :

" A woman celebrated the anniversary of her marriage. She had been a poor despised maiden when her bridegroom chose her to be his bride. He took her from her low and miserable estate

to the hearth which he had prepared for her
in the house which he had prepared for her
home. She was unfaithful to him : and, in the
foreign land whither she had gone, she celebrated her wedding day, and repeated the loving
words and narrated the acts of condescension
and tender friendship of her bridegroom ; she
boasted that she had always kept this feast for
a great number of years ; but she did not
know where her husband was ; she hardly knew
whether he was still living ; she had forgotten
his face, and did not care to see him again.
Listen to the festive song—listen to the touching
narrative of the bridegroom's affectionate and
tender wooing, his greatness and condescension.
. . . . Yes, the husband himself was listening
at the door, and said, 'She adds scorn to faith-
lessness.' . . . . 'Thou art the wife, O daughter
of Zion, thou My people, saith Jehovah, and thy
Passover feast is mockery. Despised, enslaved,
ill-treated wert thou in the land of Egypt ; and
I chose thee for My bride ; and delivered thee
with strong hand and outstretched arm, and

led thee to Mount Sinai as to the bridal altar, where I entered into covenant with thee. I led thee through the wilderness to the home which I prepared for thee, into the land flowing with milk and honey.

" 'Thou wert a loving bride to Me, and followedst Me in the wilderness, a land unsown; there wert thou Mine own. Why hast thou forsaken Me, why hast thou forgotten Me for thousands of years? Yes, thou knowest Me not, and sayest: Who is God, and who knows anything certainly about Him? and yet thou keepest our wedding day!'

"So spake the Lord. Oh! that my head were waters, and mine eyes a fountain of tears, that I might weep day and night for the misery of my people. I see how they coil their lips with ridicule; I hear them laughing in derision, how they regard me as an enthusiast and a fool, because I speak of God as the Bridegroom of Israel, because I lament that Israel does not stand in fellowship with God. Who is Jehovah? I hear them say, 'He dwells high above the starry firmament.' Let every one live according to his conscience, as he thinks proper; and others think, 'What profit is it that we keep the ancient ordinances, and live a strict life? we commend, therefore, the enlightened and free-thinkers;' and others again speak of a God in everything, without will, without love, who cannot see, hear, and help. And all forget that they, Jews, have to do, not with an unknown, hidden God, but with the God who brought them out of Egypt, who has revealed His thoughts and commandments to Israel, and is their Lord and King."

The young student looked, somewhat contemptuously, straight before him; the old man was thoughtful, and muttered softly some verses from the prophet Jeremiah, of which the passage, read from the pamphlet, reminded him:

"I remember thee, the kindness of thy youth, the love of thine espousals, when thou wentest after Me in the wilderness, in a land that was not sown ... Can a maid forget her ornaments, or a bride her attire? yet My people have forgotten Me days without number." [1]

The master of the house stared at his friend, whom he could not thoroughly understand; his wife broke the painful silence with the words:

"Dear Mr. Ernest, we should not speculate much about such sublime subjects. We get quite bewildered when we begin to think of God and the future life. It is quite dreadful, and fit to drive one mad."

"Yes," replied Ernest, "you are right; the thought of God is something oppressive to you. The consciousness of the existence of God must press with fearful weight on every one who does not know and love God as his Father in his heart. Understand me rightly. I mean something when I use these expressions. Since German essays have been delivered from the pulpits of Jewish temples, to the satisfaction of the audience, people cannot believe that religion is anything but a set of phrases. The thought

---

[1] Jeremiah ii. 2, 32.

of God is dreadful to every one who does not know and love God as his Father. Not as the Creator of the planets, the Architect of the universe, the Controller of the course of the world's history. Does a child know his father as the physician who heals the sick, the advocate who conducts cases, or the scholar who writes books? Does it not rather know him as the man whom it loves and trusts, who protects, cherishes, caresses, instructs, educates it? Are you a planet, or a mountain, or an historical event; or are you a human being, a child of God, a Jewess, a bride of Jehovah? But you do not know God."

"What do you mean by God?" asked the young philosopher. "You know that the opinions entertained on the subject are very various."

"Yes," said the master of the house, taking up the word; "what do we know of God? This much is clear, that yonder above the sky a good Father must dwell;[1] but more than this we

---

[1] Quotation from Schiller.

cannot know on earth ; and I do not see that it would be necessary."

"I see God in everything!" exclaimed madame ; "or rather I feel God ; when I hear a symphony of Beethoven, or look into the cup of a flower, or the blue sky in summer. Feeling is everything, call it bliss, love, God—name is sound and smoke." [1]

Ernest replied, "I see the question, Who is Jehovah? does not come from pagan Egypt, but from the people of Jehovah. Allow me to premise that I am no philosopher, no admirer of Goethe, no German, . . . but a Jew ; and I will have nothing whatever to do with views and opinions about God, no matter whose they may be, however celebrated the names of those who hold them, Kant, Hegel, etc., etc. It is sheer waste of time, for what we need, and must have, is truth—certainty. And this is to be got only in Judah. In Judah God is known, because He has revealed Himself to Judah. We know some-

---

[1] From Goethe's *Faust*.

thing definite about God, and not only that a good Father must live above the sky, for God has *revealed* Himself—— "

"Revealed!" exclaimed the three, with one breath. "What do you mean by that?"

"Is it not true," said Ernest, "the most insignificant man keeps his thoughts and feelings a secret, as his property, locked in his own soul? If I am to know them, not merely guess and suppose, this can only be if he communicates his thoughts and feelings to me. And shall not what applies to man apply also to God, whose thoughts are as much higher than ours as the heaven is higher than the earth? We can only know His will and His counsel when He reveals and communicates it to us. Because you do not believe in a living God who has created the eye, and Himself sees; has planted the ear, and Himself hears; who has created beings who have wills, and who Himself has will—because you do not believe in the God who has brought us out of Egypt, therefore it seems strange to you when I maintain God has spoken, God has revealed Himself."

"In every flower God reveals Himself," remarked madame.

"How," answered Ernest, "were there no flowers in Greece and Italy? Ask the Hottentot in South Africa, the Indian, who lets himself be crushed by the sacred car, what the flowers have revealed to them of God. Yes; in the most favourable case, if flowers, if nature, declares to man the existence, the power, and the wisdom of God, can the flowers answer such questions as these for you—to what end am I on earth? whither do I go after death? what does God require of me? Can flowers appease the anguish of conscience, or make the thought of God and eternity—which you have described as dreadful—more tolerable?"

Madame was silent, but her brother took up the word:

"God is to be known with the reason, in which God reveals Himself to the human spirit."

"I grant you," replied Ernest, "that God is to be known with the reason, if you understand by reason, as I do not doubt, everything that distinguishes us from the beasts. We are to know God with our reason, even as with the eye objects are seen; if I close my eye, I see nothing but glimmer and deceptive forms; for the objects are not in the eye, but only the capacity to see when the object and light are there. Just so with the reason: God is to be known by the reason; but He is not in the reason, just as little as you will see the sun if you close your eyes, which are quite sound and admirably adapted for seeing. When God reveals Himself—shows Himself—then He is to be seen with the eye of the mind. If, however, you think that you will find God in your reason, then will you think out a god for yourself; that, however, is no God, but a creature—your creature, your last essay."

"'Shall a man make gods unto himself, and they are no gods?'"[1] added the old man,

[1] Jeremiah xvi. 20.

who had listened to Ernest with great attention.

"Yes," continued Ernest; "if the eye were
not adapted to light, how could it bear the sun ?
Were we not made in the image of God, with
spiritual eyes to see Him and hearts to love
Him, revelation would be of no use to us ; but,
because we have heart and reason, woe to us if
we do not hearken to His voice and consider
His revelation. We Jews especially, and on
such a feast as to-day's, are quite without
excuse."

"It is very difficult, dear Ernest," said his
old friend, Raphael, "to believe in things that
have happened thousands of years ago."

"Not difficult," continued Ernest, "when
there is a Passover feast which proclaims the
wonderful work of God from year to year.
This festival seals and confirms it to those who
will believe ; but it must confound and condemn
the unbeliever, because it is the witness to an
historical fact, because it proves that there is a
living God. You do not believe in the God

who has spoken at Sinai—how you explain the *Gadah* I do not know,—you believe in a good Father who must be living on high, with whom you have no communion; your dear wife believes in a god who consists of sky-blue, the odour of roses, and a feeling for symphonies, call it bliss, heart, love, god; our young friend seeks God in the human mind. Now I will tell you something,—the heathens, who do not possess Moses and the Prophets, nor the Passover feast, who sought without revelation to know God, who strove to solve the problems of the heart with their philosophy, did their duty: there was no other way open to them. Jews, however, must first become apostates before they fall into the new-fashioned scepticism; must first forsake Jehovah, the fountain of living waters, before they hew themselves out broken cisterns that can hold no water; must first say to Moses— who declares to us the Word of God, 'I am the Lord thy God, who brought thee out of Egypt'—'Thou speakest untruth, and deceivest us,' before you permit yourselves to answer the

question, Who is God ? out of Goethe's *Faust.*
Suppose for a moment—I do not ask you to
believe at present—only that you put the case
hypothetically, that what you have read about
the exodus of Israel from Egypt to-day is true,
and then tell me whether God must not look
upon your keeping the Passover—and as you
keep it so do thousands of Jews—as a mockery
and a profanation of His name ? "

" You would be the last to counsel me not to
keep the Passover," said Raphael.

" Certainly," replied Ernest, " one would
rather see you act illogically, than completely
break with the covenant of God. But do not
continue in your unbelief and error, do not
continue to mock God, by reading in His
presence what His love led Him to do for
Israel, without believing it. Return to God.
Regard human views as views, and turn to the
truth, to the Word of God. Return to the old
Book. It is old as the sun is old, but ever new
in its illuminating and quickening power, in its
warmth and beauty. For thousands of years it

has been life-sustaining, strength-giving, food and refreshment to the human heart. Blessed Passover, which leads you back to God and to His Word!"

"Alas, alas, that there is so little learning among us now!" said the old family friend, Jacob, taking up the discourse. "Where do we find any one now who knows the Talmud? and how can one wonder that faith disappears?"

"Dear sir," said Ernest, "the Talmud can give no help. It was written only by men. You think by wise and pious men. I do not at present dispute this. But that has nothing to do with the matter. They were only fallible men, who often did err and who contradict one another. Now it amounts to much about the same thing, whether one depends on the views of old Rabbis and learned men, or of modern Rabbis and philosophers; whether one relies on what Rabbi Akiba, Rabbi Eliezer, or what Mendelsohn, Lessing, or Goethe declares. God has spoken, כה אמר יהוה. Thus saith the Lord.

In the Word of God, in the Scripture [תנך] is truth; in the Talmud human views (often false, contradictory, repulsive, as you know better than I do)."

"Yes," answered Jacob; "but look you, the right exposition of Holy Scripture is not so easy; much learning, much study is necessary for that; and in the Talmud we have the exposition of the wisest and most learned men who have lived in Israel."

The stranger reflected for a moment.

"I might easily show you," said he, "how the Talmudical expositions of the Bible often fail to explain the sense, but rather pervert and distort it. But it is not at all needful for my purpose. The Talmud, we will admit, contains the most solid wisdom, a correct, reasonable, learned exposition of the Word of God. I maintain, we do not *need* such an exposition. The Word of God is intelligible, and makes the simple wise; what God has given to men to enlighten and bless them—to men, mark you, not to *Chachamim*, the subtle, but men, women, and children—does not need folios of learned and subtle expositions, over which every one is not able to pore. The sun does not require any wax candles to help us to see it. The people to whom Moses and Ezra read the law understood it without Raschi, and King David went to God, and not to Jarchi, with the prayer, 'Open Thou mine eyes, that I may behold wondrous things out of Thy law.' [1]

"This Talmud, with its 'Rabbi A— says,' and its 'Rabbi N— says,' has no value for me; the Tenach, with its 'Thus saith the Lord,' is everything to me. There may be beautiful stories, ingenious similitudes, in these old Talmudic books. But God says by Jeremiah; 'The prophet that hath a dream, let him tell a dream; and he that hath My Word, let him speak My Word faithfully. What is the chaff to the wheat? saith the Lord. Is not my Word like as a fire? saith the Lord; and like a hammer that breaketh the rock in pieces?' [2]

[1] Psalm cxix. 18.　　　　[2] Jer. xxiii. 28, 29.

" According to your view, women and unlearned people generally cannot themselves know God's truth and will, but must constantly be dependent on their Rabbis and teachers. There is not a trace of this in Holy Scripture. On the contrary, is it not everywhere maintained in the Scriptures that the Word of God is near to every one, that it—God's Word, *not* the exposition—makes the simple wiser and more prudent than the *Chachamim?*

" The Talmudists have fallen away from the God of Israel and His truth, as well as the so-called Enlightened and Reformed. For centuries the voice in Israel was always heard, ' Thus saith the Lord.' For eighteen hundred years this exclamation has been no longer heard in Israel. Since then it is said, ' Thus says Rabbi A—, and Rabbi N—; ' and in more recent times, ' So says this philosopher or that.' Either the story that is told in the תנך is not true, or it happened in some other world, or these eighteen hundred years are the long period of which it is said in the דברי הימים

there will be no true God in Israel, and which Hosea has described." [1]

"Pray," said the old friend of the family, "have you studied the Talmud?"

"Dear sir," replied Ernest, "did I not grant to you that the Talmud contains the most solid wisdom? Yet I will have nothing to say about the Talmud. I will have nothing to do with it. Show me why I ought to read the Talmud. Show me what more claim the Talmud has on my time, attention, and respect than Mendelssohn's works, or any other modern book? Why will you drive me continually away from the Word of Jehovah, the תנך, to the Talmud? Do you know why? For the same reason that makes friends Raphael and Abraham urge me to read Lessing, Kant, and other authors, instead of the תנך. You are afraid of God. You are afraid that there is such a thing as firm, definite truth ; and you would like to hide yourselves in the thousand and one views and opinions and suppositions of Rabbis and men of genius.

[1] Hosea iii. 1, 3. Compare 2 Chron. xv. 3.

" You won't have the תנך, because you won't have God, who speaks therein."

The philosopher rose up at these words, looked at his watch, and thought it was high time for him to go home. The old friend, however, wished to remain longer, and have some more conversation with the stranger, who appeared now to be a " good Jew," and again, " not to be a good Jew." It was agreed, at last, to meet again next evening.

Before they parted, however, Ernest read the following parable:

" There was once a man, whose sons lost their liberty by their frivolity, and fell into a grievous captivity in a foreign land. The father's heart could not endure the thought of their being in such distress, and resolved to free them. He betook himself into the foreign country, and when he had bound the gaoler hand and foot, he threw the key through the grating, and called out, ' Dear children, let yourselves out, and come home with me. I will pardon your levity, I will forgive your disobedience.' It was, however, a cold winter morning, and a heavy shower of snow was falling. The sons sat down, looked at the key, and conversed about the size and shape of it, and the invention of the locksmith's art. Some praised the happiness of freedom, as the greatest and most indispensable boon; they described the peace and comfort of the father's house. 'There,' said the father, 'the key is for opening; you have no time to lose.' But they lingered over it, looking at the key and speaking about it; and some of them thought that the key would never do, it was too small, something must be filed away from the ward on one side and added to it on the other. They did it; but, behold, it would no more answer its purpose. But they cried, 'Now it is a decent key! We have so perfected the key that we are wiser and more skilful than the original locksmith; what were his work without our improvement?' But the key would not do; the door remained shut. Then the father said, tears filling his eyes, 'You won't return home! Ye do not love me, and would rather stay in prison than listen to me.' They replied, 'Nothing is more beautiful, nothing more worthy of a man, nothing is higher and holier than filial love and veneration.' Thereupon the father continued earnestly and mournfully, 'If you really loved me, you would have opened the door long ago.' But there were some of them who mocked, and laughed, and said, 'The key is no key at all; and what need have we of any ? It is very pleasant, and a man can make himself quite happy here. True freedom is not to be found at home. Are we not free ?' "

"This is the story," concluded Ernest, "and the application——"

"Come," said young Abraham to the old man; "we two are meant, you the Talmudist, and I the free-thinker. Good night !"

Second Evening.

Our friends met again on the following evening in Raphael's house. The old man had the Hagadah lying before him, and reminded Ernest of his promise to continue the conversation begun yesterday.

"I cannot comprehend," said the mistress of the house, "how people can take any interest in religious controversy. I respect every conscientious conviction; but I think if every one adheres firmly to what he knows and believes, if every one lives according to his views, then he is blessed in them. Let me have my belief; I let you have yours."

"Pardon me," said Ernest, "if I answer your remark without reserve. If what you say about religion were applied to any other subject, you yourself would perceive how senseless and false it is. If any one maintained—'You are of opinion that fire burns, beware of putting your fingers in the fire ; but if you do not share the conviction, fire will ·not hurt you : whoever does what he knows and believes of nature is quite safe, and no harm will befal him ;—you would say at once, ‘The man is a dreamer ; he does not know that there are laws of nature.’ Now, I declare you, misguided friend, to be a great dreamer who does not consider that the laws of the spiritual world are much more certain and unalterable than those of the outward visible one; and that you, as a Jewess, cannot plead the excuse of ignorance, for God has revealed these laws to us Jews. I see you do not understand me rightly. Suppose a wise, excellent, and experienced man had lived some months ago in this street, though I did not know it, and I were told that if I had visited him he would have received me in a friendly manner. Suppose I ·said I knew nothing of it, and therefore I have lost nothing. Would the circumstance that I knew nothing of the man be a compensation for the pleasure and profit which his acquaintance would have afforded me?

Certainly not; and what should I think of the friend, who knew the man, and did not take me to him? Might I not justly accuse him of indolence and neglect? Don't you see that I should be a negligent, indolent, and faithless friend, if I did not direct you, however irksome it might be to you, to one who lives near you, and is only waiting for you to come to Him, even Jehovah, the God of Israel? You have not yet sought Him, and therefore you have not found Him. He is not to be found in *Faust*, or in a symphony, or in hyacinths. I cannot leave you alone in your faith, as you call it, because you have no faith. Views, suppositions, can make no claim to the name of faith. I believe what God has said, therefore I speak."

"Yes," said Raphael; "I understand that. If I thought, as Ernest does, that God Himself reveals the way to blessedness—if, like him, I were firmly convinced that the Bible is really the Word of God, I should hold it to be my duty to win all my acquaintances to my opinion."

"Ah," said Abraham, "where does any one

live who shares these views? Reflect that we live in the nineteenth century—that Galileo, Rousseau, Kant, Lessing have not laboured in vain : who that claims to have any culture, and to understand the spirit of the times, would waste his time in such mediæval discussion?"

"If you would see the old-fashioned man," said Ernest, "who believes the Bible, even after the invention of printing and the barometer, and after the French Revolution, you have now that pleasure. Since you have spoken of the spirit of the times, I would remind you that in every age, from the beginning hitherto, two different spirits have animated men. It was the spirit of the age that cast and worshipped the golden calf; it was the spirit of the age, not so long ago, that carried a profligate woman to the temple as the representative of the Deity; and from century to century this spirit will animate men, and ever anew produce men of intellectual power and of genius. Yea, this tendency will ever advance more consistently, more boldly, more audaciously. But, dear philosopher, side by side with all these phenomena, a people lives for thousands of years, which, to some extent against its will, is a visible, palpable proof that Jehovah is King in heaven, and that His truth confounds all lies ; this people, itself fallen from Jehovah, scattered abroad in all lands, testifies— an impartial witness, for it testifies against itself— that God has revealed Himself, and His Word is truth—firm as a rock; that all that is foretold in it meets its fulfilment. You, sir, have the honour to belong to this people, whose destiny and history was a dark enigma to your omniscient Hegel, and must be a dark enigma to every one who does not know Jehovah as the living God, who does not live in the same fellowship with Him as Abraham, David, and all believers of the old covenant. I told you yesterday that I am no philosopher, that neither the nineteenth century, Goethe, nor any man of genius is my idol. I am a Jew; I know the truth ; Jehovah has revealed it, and I have experienced it in my heart."

There was something in the decided, solemn

tone, and still more in the earnest, affectionate, and melancholy countenance of Ernest, that struck Abraham, and drew him powerfully to the remarkable stranger. In a less confident tone he asked, "Does not the Hagadah appear to you to be really insipid, antiquated, and, for our time, senseless? Rabbi Joses' fifty plagues, for example; because one finger denotes ten plagues, hence it follows that the Hand of God denotes fifty. That is just one point that occurs to me. And then what sense can there be in saying: 'To-day here, a year hence in Jerusalem?' In my opinion, one had better say, a year hence in Spain![1] To what purpose this antiquated idea, which is such a favourite one among our opponents—the enemies of emancipation?"

"It is not my business," replied Ernest, "to defend what Rabbi Jose and Rabbi Akiba say; because their opinions, just like the opinions of

---

[1] At the time this pamphlet was written, the re-admission of the Jews into Spain was spoken of.

other men, have no authority, save in so far as they agree with the Word of God. As regards the passage, however, 'To-day here, next year in Palestine,' it is clear to every one who believes that Jehovah led His people out of Egypt, that He will one day bring back His people out of all lands whither He has scattered them, and restore them to their own land. As long as the deliverance from Egypt is not a living certainty in your heart, but is regarded by you only as an old legend, a venerable tradition, you can only treat the expectation of the restoration of the Jewish nation as an antiquated idea. You must first return to Jehovah, acknowledge the God who brought our fathers out of Egypt, then you will become a Jew, and see what a great and glorious future is in store for the Jewish nation. I emphasize the word 'nation,' for you wish the nation to cease; you think that the Jews have reached the summit when they are incorporated with other nations in the various countries of the world, and single individuals distinguish themselves, and become great actors, poets, composers, etc. The prophetic Word, and the true Israelite, however, look forward to a restoration—a union of the Jewish nation. ' If I forget thee, O Jerusalem, let my right hand forget her cunning.' Allow me, as briefly as possible, to recal to you the history of the first Passover which was celebrated in Israel— we shall then understand each other better."

"No sermon," said the mistress of the house, in a lively manner ; " we had one already this forenoon."

"No," continued Ernest ; "I will only set before you the truths which I have apprehended, and show that you celebrate no true Passover— that you have fallen away from Jehovah the God of Israel, and beseech you to return to Him. There is this fundamental difference between me and the Jewish preachers : they always speak to the greatest satisfaction of their hearers, strengthen and encourage them to virtuous effort, etc. ; I, on the contrary, declare to them, in the most decided and solemn manner, that they have departed from the right way, and must undergo a thorough change if they would please God and be blessed. Because I would convince you of this, I beg you to interrupt me if anything is unintelligible and offensive to you, and speak out your objections as plainly as I make my attack."

They were satisfied with this explanation and proposal, and Ernest began :

" The children of Israel were in ignominious and grinding servitude.   Mindful of the promise that God had given to Abraham, that He would make him the father of a great people, He had compassion on Israel, and stirred up Moses to emancipate them.   Moses and Aaron go to Pharaoh, and call upon him, in the name of Jehovah, to let the people go.   The Egyptian king, who is not willing to relax his cruel unrighteousness, asks proudly and scornfully : ' Who is Jehovah, that I should obey Him ? ' Then God shows His power.   The king refuses to believe, even after these proofs.   The signs are therefore changed into *plagues ;* if, peradventure, he may be moved, through fear of

the punishment of this Almighty Being, to bow
before Him.   At the bidding of Moses, plagues
come up out of the healthful waters of Egypt,
and out of the fruitful Nile valley (the river-
god—Father Nile; the soil, the deified power
of nature); plagues came from the bright
atmosphere that surrounds the land.   When
Egypt's own nature is exhausted, neighbouring
lands contribute their plagues: from the Arabian
desert came the locusts: from the Sahara, scorch-
ing wind, with impenetrable darkness.   Thus
Jehovah revealed Himself, that He is Lord in
the midst of the earth, Lord of water, air, and
earth, over so-called gods, men, cattle, and
plants, and that there is none like Him." [1]

Here the mistress of the house interrupted
him, and asked how it was possible to see such
wonders, and not believe; whether this was not
in and of itself a proof that the history is not
really true?

"The wonders that Jehovah permits," replied

---

[1] Exodus viii. 22; ix. 14.

Ernest, "do not compel belief; they are all of a
kind that leave belief or unbelief a matter of
free choice. What would be the value of a
forced belief? The plagues were all announced
beforehand by Moses; it was, therefore, clear
that they proceeded from the God of Moses.

"Whoever would not believe, however—as
for instance Pharaoh, who would not believe
because he was not ready to obey God and give
up his tyranny over the Jews—he could, of course,
shrug his shoulders, and say, 'They are remarkable natural phenomena; we cannot, it is true,
explain them; but we do not know what they
signify.' So it is nowadays. The predictions
of the prophets have been fulfilled in the most
remarkable manner. I see in this the clearest
visible proof that Jehovah has sent the prophets,
that His Word is true. You say, It is remarkable, a singular coincidence, and so on. We sit
here together on the second Passover evening.
That is a miracle—that we Jews, scattered over
the whole earth, exist, in spite of all persecutions;
and everything that Moses and the prophets

predict about us is fulfilled. More remarkable than Pharaoh's unbelief is the fact that you, a Jewess, still occupy the same ground as Pharaoh, and ask: Who is Jehovah? Is not one religious opinion as good as another? This, in a preliminary way, in answer to your question. After God, in His long-suffering, had given them opportunity to turn to Him, He sends them the tenth and last plague. He does not call forth the staff of Moses: the starting-point now is not water, air, and earth, but the Hand of Jehovah interferes directly."

" ' About midnight will I go out into the midst of Egypt and smite all the first-born of men and beasts, and will execute judgment on the gods of Egypt: I, Jehovah, will do it; but against any of the children of Israel shall not a dog move his tongue, that ye may know how that the Lord doth put a difference between the Egyptians and Israel.'

" On the evening of the fourteenth day of the month Nisan a lamb without blemish must be slain, and the upper door-posts, and the side posts were to be sprinkled with the blood, in order that when Jehovah goes through the land to slay the firstborn, the avenging angel pass by all the houses that had this sign of expiation, namely, the blood. The Israelite who slaughtered the lamb knew that he, as well as the Egyptians, had sinned, and deserved the Divine punishment, and received deliverance from the Divine judgment, not as a consequence of his own worthiness and merit, but from the grace of God alone. And God in His mercy promised that He would accept the blood of the guiltless lamb (blood is the seat of life, Leviticus xvii. 14) instead of the blood, that is, life of the sinner, and would remit the punishment. The blood of expiation, therefore, is what distinguishes Israel from Egypt; and the atoning blood of the Passover lamb is the token to all times of the God of Israel; for not only in Egypt ought this lamb to be offered, but God commands: [1]

"'Kill the Passover. For the Lord will pass

----

[1] Exodus xii. 21, 24.

through to smite the Egyptians; and when He
seeth the blood upon the lintel, and on the two
side posts, the Lord will pass over. . . . . Ye
shall observe this thing for an ordinance to
thee and to thy sons for ever.'

"Herein consists the second apostasy of Israel;
as they forsake Jehovah, they no longer have
that which distinguishes Jehovah's people from
other people—the blood of the Passover lamb.
The holy Jehovah can only then take sinful
Israel for His people when her sin is atoned; for
the Passover lamb is the foundation of all sin-
offerings that God afterwards instituted."

"In my opinion," said Raphael, interrupting
the speaker, "sacrifices were only outward
tokens of gratitude; the readiness of the people
to serve the Lord with all their power was
expressed by them."

"True," answered Ernest, "there were such
offerings also; but, you see, the Passover lamb
was not one of them. And it is impossible to
deny that God instituted sacrifices through
Moses, in virtue of which sin was atoned for

and forgiven. Be so good as to read the Old Testament as attentively as another book, and to extract its contents from the book, not to import them into it. You are always free to believe it or not. If you read the books of Moses, you will find that the law which God gave to His people was so clear a mirror that even the dullest eyes could see their sins in it. The anger of Jehovah against all unrighteousness and sin is so clearly expressed in the threatenings and the curse which are denounced against every transgressor, that God in His love and compassion instituted sacrifices for the expiation of sin. Thus God is righteous and holy—sin is punished: He is gracious and compassionate, ' He willeth not the death of a sinner, but rather that he should turn unto Him and live.' "

" Pardon me," said Abraham; " that is a heathenish idea. According to your representation, God is cruel, and must be appeased by an offering."

" Not so, dear friend," maintained Ernest;

" God Himself institutes the offering ; determines in the most exact way its character and method ; gives His people the means of atonement ; shows, therefore, that He is a God of love—that He does not hate the sinner, but the sin."

Abraham would not accept this explanation ; he did not advance anything more, however, in reply to it, but that the heathen also had their sacrifices.

" There is nothing strange in that. It only shows that the heathen as well as the Jews were created in the image of God, had a conscience, which told them that sin (as in German the word itself indicates;[1] in Hebrew חטאת is both sin and sin-offering) must be atoned for. Suppose there were two children in a family, Charles and Emil, both of whom had been naughty, and Charles wished to make reparation, but set about it in a wrong way; this would still show that he had a filial heart.

[1] Sünde—sin ; sühnen—atone.

Suppose, on the contrary, Emil said, 'What is the use of making such a commotion about my disobedience to my old father?' he would show that the last traces of filial reverence and love were obliterated from his heart. Therefore the heathen with their hecatombs occupy a far higher ground than the Illuminati of the nineteenth century, who show no concern about the forgiveness of their sins."

"Yet," said Raphael, "is not God the most perfect love—love itself? why should He not forgive us all?"

"Dear friend," said Ernest, "you are right —God is love. But we must know who God is, and what love signifies. If you only mean God is love in the sense that He is indulgent, and will not look so narrowly into the matter, but pass over transgressions of His holy law, you know neither who God is nor what love is. God, who has in Himself all blessedness, created all worlds and beings in order to manifest His glory, and that hearts might feel and respond to His love. All men on earth, united to Him

in love, were designed to lead a pure and happy
life. The relationship between God and man
was designed to be like the relationship between
father and child, husband and wife—in affection,
tenderness, and living communion. This kingdom of peace and harmony exists no longer.
We know that instead of it, selfishness, cruelty,
envy, hatred, are active among us; every one
knows by his own experience that he does not
stand in the child-like relationship to God in
which Adam formerly stood—sin has done that.
But sin is something that does not come from
God, but from ourselves: therefore we have
shut ourselves out of the kingdom of heaven.
What comfort is it for me to know now God is
love? He willed thy happiness, He did all for
thee; but thou hast wilfully gone out of this
kingdom of love. God is love; this cannot
signify that God loves this or that individual—
no, He is love itself: He wills the good, the
pure—whatever brings health, blessing, joy, life.
But what produces curse, death, envy, hatred,
is contrary to the love of God: the love of God

must reveal itself as anger against every un-righteous being. The righteousness of God is nothing else but the love of God that opposes everything corrupt. Punishment follows sin: the conscience of the man created in the image of God recognizes this law to be a righteous one. The love of God is, therefore, no pacifying thought for the sinner, but a two-edged sword. The other edge of the sword I will show you presently.

"Just because God is love He wills our love, and that such only should be with Him who return His love; were God not love, He would perhaps be content that, depending on the pursuits, joys, and gifts of earth, we should never think of Him, and, at most, laud Him on a rare occasion with high-soaring phrases as the Creator of the planets, that we should gladly remain on earth for ever, and that the state after death—immediate fellowship with God—should not be the subject either of thought or of desire. God is love; but those who will not permit themselves to be loved by Him, who do not love Him, are like an adulterous wife, who, unfaithful to her husband, says, ' My husband loves me most tenderly.' How can she speak so without tears of penitence and shame choking her voice, the heartless wife ? "

This simile seemed absurd in the highest degree to the company. Ernest noticed it, and added :

" An offence against æsthetics is the greatest sin in your eyes.   You think this simile absurd in the highest degree ; it is not to be found in modern poetry, but in the Old Testament, which is concentrated in this simile—Thy Creator is thine husband; Israel, who goes after idols, is an adulteress: as a wife is to her husband, so is Israel to Jehovah in love and subjection.   God chose the Jewish people for a bride to Himself; He redeemed her out of Egypt, He loved her first, atoned for her with the Paschal lamb. They accepted His love, brought the Paschal offering, and sprinkled the door-posts with its blood.   But you are an apostate from Jehovah ;

despised is His grace—rejected is His offering of reconciliation, and you mock Him by speaking of His love."

"Dear sir," said old Jacob, "do you not know that we serve God, and hope to obtain pardon by repentance, almsgiving, and prayer? Have we not a *Jom Kippur?*"[1]

"Yes, indeed," replied Ernest, "you have *Jom Kippur*, prayers, almsgiving; you have everything in the world, only not Jehovah; you will tolerate everything, only not the love of God; you will make compensation for your sins in all possible ways; only you will not seek forgiveness in the way Jehovah has commanded. God says, 'The soul that sinneth it shall not do penance, pray, give alms,—no, it shall die, it is guilty of death.' All the money in the world, all the fasting, cannot compensate for sin; and in the *Jom Kippur* itself, in the day, there is no atoning power. 'The blood have I given you upon the altar to make

---

[1] Day of atonement.

an atonement for your souls; for it is the blood
that maketh an atonement for the soul,'[1] not
the *Jom Kippur*, that has four-and-twenty
hours, and is a day like any other.

"Dear friend, a heart that acknowledges its
sin and fears the punishment of God, which
feels how sin has estranged it from God, and
therefore made it unhappy, cannot quietly wait
until the *Jom Kippur* returns. But that is just
the point, *that* you do not feel that you are
sinners. Look here—David felt his sins as a
heavy load that was too burdensome for him:
'My transgressions are more than the hairs of
my head; I cry by reason of the disquietude
of my heart.' Isaiah calls out, 'Woe is me!
for I am undone; for I am a man of unclean
lips.' Can you speak of such anxiety and
disquietude, such pain and woe, which you
have felt on account of your sins? Either you
are so much better, more God-fearing, pious
than David and Isaiah; or these men saw

[1] Lev. xvii. 11.

something which is concealed from you. I will
tell you briefly what you lack,—you have no
Jehovah, and therefore do not know what it is
to feel pain for sin. No one can feel sin against
the pantheistic God—the all,—nor against the
Architect of the universe; only against the
Father, the King, the Covenant-God, Jehovah.
Isaiah saw Jehovah sitting on a throne, high
and lifted up, and heard the praise of the
Seraphim, 'Holy, holy, holy, art Thou Lord
of hosts!' And then he called out, 'Woe is
me! I am undone, I am a sinful, unclean man!'
That is why some do not feel sin as such.
Others," continued Ernest, turning to the old
friend of the family, "fear punishment, but
have no desire to come to God. Jehovah,
moreover, is an unknown God to them. The
bride who offends her bridegroom, and therefore
is banished from him, will never rest until
she sees him again, receives assurance of forgiveness from his lips, rests on his bosom. She
desires forgiveness of her wrong only as a
means to an end; she desires himself above all

things. 'My soul longeth for Thee, O God,' says David.

"The bride will not say, 'I have written twenty letters to my bridegroom—so touching, so humble, so affectionate; I have done this and that; now I am content; what more can be asked of me?' No; but she will go into the town where he dwells, and fulfil all the conditions which he imposes, in order to her restoration. You are contented with your prayers, your emotions, your righteousnesses; therefore you will have nothing to do with the only means that God Himself has instituted?"

"How can we now offer sacrifices?" said Jacob; "we have no temple, no high priest. You demand an impossibility."

" I demand no impossibility," replied Ernest. " But Jehovah commands the Paschal lamb to be offered, and the blood to be sprinkled on the door-posts. Our fathers were to do this, and their children after them for ever and ever."

"But you know," said Jacob, " as well as I do, that God cannot ask anything impossible from us."

"God will not contradict Himself," answered Ernest. "Therefore I must search and try how this contradiction may be explained. Listen to me, I pray you. The sacrifices which our fore-fathers offered in obedience to God's command, set before their eyes in a lively manner the truth that God cannot permit sin to go unpunished, that it must be atoned for; and that He accepted the life of the beast instead of the life of the sinner. The Israelite saw in the sacrifice, on the one side, how guilty and damnable sin is, and that Jehovah is gracious and full of com-passion. But these sacrifices had to be yearly offered; and this circumstance alone shows that the sacrifice itself could not atone for sin. The sacrifices were only types and prophecies of the One offering, pure and spotless, sinless and innocent, who consciously, and of His own will, should take upon Himself the sins of the people, and atone for them by His death. Isaiah was one of the Israelites into whose heart this concrete prophecy, the Paschal Lamb, penetrated deeply; he saw in spirit the true Paschal Lamb, the Servant of God, the Messiah. 'He was led as a lamb to the slaughter; and as a sheep before her shearers is dumb, so He opened not His mouth.' 'But He was wounded for our transgressions, He was bruised for our iniquities: the chastisement of our peace was upon Him; and with His stripes we are healed.'[1]

"When the servant of Jehovah, the מלאך הברית for whom our fathers longed, came to His temple,[2] then Jochanan, the son of the priest Zachariah, cried out, 'Behold the Lamb of God, that taketh away the sin of the world.' And at the feast of Passover, He was led to the slaughter, and opened not His mouth; when He was oppressed and afflicted, and gave His body, not a bone of which was broken, for our sins, and shed His blood for our iniquities. And as He died the veil of the temple was rent, the Messiah was cut off, but not for Himself, but for us, reconciliation was made for

---

[1] Isaiah liii.   [2] Mal. iii. 1.

iniquity, and everlasting righteousness brought in. [1]

"This is the true Paschal Lamb, offered once for all; whoever believes on Him, looking for forgiveness of his sins to Him alone, the Lamb of God, the Anointed, who shed His blood for sinners, has his heart sprinkled with the blood of atonement; he belongs to the Israel of God. Behold how the command of God is no impossible one : 'Keep it, thou and thy children for ever.' We have a Paschal Lamb, namely, Joshua the Messiah, who Himself bare our griefs, and carried our sorrows. When the sun shines, the moon pales. When the fruit matures, the blossom withers; the Holy Anointed One has been slain for the iniquity of His people: animal sacrifices cease."

"All this is so new and strange," said Jacob, " I know not what to think of it. I have often wondered at the fact that we cannot keep the law of Moses, especially when I see how the

[1] Daniel ix. 24, 26.

reforming Jews cast off, on that account, so much of our Scripture. We are in captivity, and, therefore, have no temple, altar, and sacrifice."

"No," continued Ernest; "not because we are in captivity are we without the Paschal Lamb, but because we do not accept the Paschal Lamb are we in captivity. The law cannot remain; just as little as the moon remains visible when the sun rises. Show a child an apple tree in blossom, and take it to the same tree in some months, when its boughs are covered with apples. The child will seek the tree with its white and red blossoms, and be quite astonished if you say to it, 'This tree, from which I now pluck an apple for you, is the same you saw some months ago.' Just so is it with the law of Moses. It is given for ever and ever; but in its fulfilment, in its completeness, it has a different aspect from when it was in bloom. The sacrifices for sin disappeared when the true Sacrifice, the true Lamb, suffered for us at the Passover feast; the high priest who, at the *Jom Kippur*, went into the holiest of all, in order to atone for his own sins and for the sins of his people, is no longer in Israel, because the true, the only High Priest, is come, to whom God has sworn, ' Thou art a priest for ever.' [1]

" A king shall never fail upon the throne of David. Kings rule no longer in Zion ; but the Son of David, whom God has set upon His holy hill, whom David himself calls Lord, rules to all eternity, as it is written.[2]

" You seek the tree; but the tree with the buds is gone. You do not notice that the tree that has come to maturity is the same tree that bore blossoms at an earlier time. If you see Him who is the Passover Lamb לְעוֹלָם, the Cohén (priest) לְעוֹלָם, the King David לְעוֹלָם, when you acknowledge Him, then, dear friend, you will at once understand the history of Israel, the Word of God. You will acknowledge that Jehovah has disappeared from Israel for eighteen hundred years ; even His name is no more named

---

[1] Psalm cx. 4.   [2] Psalm cx. 1.

(instead of it, Adonai is used, and in the translation, the word Eternal, a cold abstraction, that never warms the heart). That these eighteen hundred years are the long time of which Hosea has said, that the children of Israel would be without temple, king, priest, ephod, and sanctuary, and, what is much worse, without Jehovah. For when Hosea adds, 'then they will *seek* Jehovah and David their King,' it follows that they have not had Him for a long time."

"If only Rabbi M—— were here!" exclaimed Jacob.

"And if Rabbi M—— and ten thousand Rabbis were here," continued Ernest, "who knew the Gemara by heart, and could expound and twist every passage of the Bible in twenty ways, what then? Would you allow these ten thousand Rabbis to determine by vote what is true, and what is not true? I have nothing to do with any Rabbi. Woe to the false prophets who give out their own dreams and subtleties for the Word of God, and say, 'God has sent us,' and it is not true. Liars are they. 'My people, they which lead thee cause thee to err, and destroy the way of thy paths.' Seducers are they, 'and they that are led of them are destroyed.'[1]

"God's Word only has authority; let us hear the Voice: Thus saith Jehovah!

"Forsake Him not; 'To-day, if ye will hear His voice, harden not your heart.' Let the Rabbis and their wisdom alone; return to Jehovah and to King David—that is, Messiah, who died for us at the Passover. Then will God heal your backsliding, love you freely, and turn away His anger from us! The time is coming, it is nigh, when Israel will return again to her God, and forsake idols, whether they be Talmud, culture, emancipation, philosophy, and turn to Him who brought them out of Egypt, who is their glory. The apostates will return to their King: then Jehovah will be as dew to His people—Israel will blossom as a rose.

[1] Isaiah iii. 12; ix. 16.

Truly I have heaviness and sorrow in my heart on your account, my brethren, my kinsfolk; and my daily prayer is that you may be saved at last from your darkness and your unbelief. Therefore I shall never cease to pray and beseech you; come and see how gracious the Lord is! As it is said in the Hallel, 'The stone which the builders rejected, the same is become the head stone of the corner.' Jesus, whom the chiefs of the people slew, is risen again; He is the כהן לעולם, the King David, לעולם, the Priest and King eternally. Blessed is he who puts his trust in Him![1] Woe to him who rejects Him!"

"That demands mature consideration," said Raphael; "it is not easy to believe it all. You are almost the only one in the town who speaks in this manner."

"True," said Ernest, "it demands mature consideration; any amount of mature consideration will avail nothing if you do not call on

[1] Hos. xiv. Ps. cx. 1, 4. Ps. ii. 12.

the God of Israel, and pray to Him : ' Give me light; open mine eyes; teach me Thy truth ! ' God will hear your prayer."

So ended the conversation.

Dear Jewish reader, if you do not know Jehovah, and King David the Messiah, you are an apostate. Turn again to Jehovah; so will He have mercy on you; seek our God, and He will abundantly pardon.

"Whom have I in heaven but Thee ? and there is none upon earth that I desire beside Thee. My flesh and my heart faileth : but God is the strength of my heart, and my portion for ever. For, lo, they that are far from Thee shall perish : Thou hast destroyed all them that go a whoring from Thee. But it is good for me to draw near to God : I have put my trust in the Lord God, that I may declare all Thy works." [1]

[1] Ps. lxxiii. 25-28.

LONDON :
PRINTED BY W. J. PERRY,
CURSITOR STREET.